Bibliographical Series
of Supplements to 'British Book News'
on Writers and Their Work

★

GENERAL EDITOR
Bonamy Dobrée

¶ HILAIRE BELLOC was born on 27 July 1870 at St. Cloud, Paris. He died on 16 July 1953 at Guildford, Surrey.

HILAIRE BELLOC
from a drawing of 1948 by JAMES GUNN
reproduced by his kind permission.

HILAIRE BELLOC

By RENÉE HAYNES

PUBLISHED FOR
THE BRITISH COUNCIL
and the NATIONAL BOOK LEAGUE
BY LONGMANS, GREEN & CO., LONDON, NEW YORK, TORONTO

LONGMANS, GREEN & CO. LTD.
6 & 7 Clifford Street, London W.1
Thibault House, Thibault Square, Cape Town
606–611 Lonsdale Street, Melbourne, C.1.

LONGMANS, GREEN & CO. INC.
55 Fifth Avenue, NEW YORK 3

LONGMANS, GREEN & CO.
20 Cranfield Road, Toronto 16

ORIENT LONGMANS PRIVATE LTD.
Calcutta   Bombay   Madras
Delhi   Hyderabad   Dacca

First published in 1953
Reprinted 1958

Printed in Great Britain by Unwin Brothers Limited
Woking and London

HILAIRE BELLOC

I

AMONG the ruling classes of England the romanticism
of the early nineteenth century, with its exquisite
sensibilities, its urgent religious feeling, its passion
for social justice, had settled down by the end of Queen
Victoria's reign into the state of a Dr. Pangloss with a stiff
upper lip; a Dr. Pangloss who concealed his feelings to such
an extent as to consider it almost indecent ('not good form',
in the parlance of the day) to envisage the existence, among
his own kind, of love, hunger, poverty, anxiety, anger, or
the desire for God. To those of other, inferior, sorts, who
exposed themselves to germs, emotions, and insecurity his
attitude was one either of condemnation or of domineering
patronage.

This was the atmosphere of the England in which Belloc
grew up; and like his contemporaries Shaw, Chesterton,
and Wells he reacted fiercely against it. These four men, of
whom two inherited a French, one an Irish, and one a
struggling-small-shopkeeper tradition, were united in the
desire to shatter the complacency of the British wealthy,
whether it were apathetic or bustling; the well-off (it was
not quite nice to call them the Rich, so Belloc invariably
did so) who existed in a kind of overstuffed, superfatted
innocence, unspoiled, some of them, by the economic world,
taking it for granted that cleanliness was next to godliness
and solvency to virtue, and that the respectability which
now glazed over earnest rationalism as well as the Established
Church obliterated even the possibility of a multitude of
sins.

All four writers, instinct with enormous vitality, set out
to shock, Shaw by rationalist and Chesterton by Christian
paradox, Wells by angry, comic, compassionate fiction, and
Belloc by satire of much that was assumed to be good, by
an exuberant boastfulness that deliberately outraged all the
current canons of gentlemanly modesty, and by a marmoreal

reassertion of Catholic belief made, not with the familiar
dazzled joy of the convert, but with the even slightly sardonic acceptance and challenge of a man long aware, and
aware with laughter, of the way in which its demands may
gall human imperfection.

His enormous output of work falls roughly into seven
overbrimming and interleaking categories. There are the
books of mockery, high spirited, genial, fierce, or bitter,
expressing itself in fiction like *The Green Overcoat* and *The
Mercy of Allah*, in spoof biographies such as *Lambkin's
Remains*, and in the collections of comic verse, *A Moral
Alphabet*, *Cautionary Tales*, *Peers*, and *More Peers*, and *The
Modern Traveller* with its virtuous and self-congratulatory
reflection that

> . . . we have got
> The Maxim Gun, and They have not.

There are the books written upon the theme summed up in
The Servile State (1912) that the great modern industrial
States are organizing their workers into a slavery which may
be more comfortable or less, but is always without roots and
without power whether its label reads 'socialist' or 'capital-
ist'; and that to restore men to the happiness and dignity
of responsible freedom it is necessary to organize the wide-
spread distribution of small property and of shares in both
the finance and the direction of communally owned public
services. This theme, originally foreshadowed in the Papal
encyclical *De Rerum Novarum* of 1880, has during the
last thirty years been worked out in very different contexts
and from very different points of view, notably by Aldous
Huxley and by Mahatma Gandhi. In the England of 1912
the suggestion was considered fantastic, and the remedy as
'reactionary' as Cobbett.

There are the historical studies, mainly concerned with
England and with France, which, some critics hold, fulfil too
well Jane Austen's criterion of perfection in this branch of

literature, inasmuch as they are 'passionate, partial, and prejudiced'; works of art rather than of scientific truth; essays in which the facts are so deeply moulded into a pre-conceived pattern of thought as to lose identity and signifi-cance. The points thus raised are open to discussion; but that discussion should not be carried on without awareness of three things. First, of course, that it has long been passion-ately debated whether history should be an art or a science, the product of a muse or of a museum. Second, that even the most conscientiously impartial of historians must, if he is a man and not an animated card-index, possess some point of view from which, willy-nilly, his work must be conceived and written. Third, that the historical point of view prevalent among Belloc's elders and contemporaries was that expressed in the baroque rocking-horse rhythms of Gibbon, the elegant inaccuracies of Macaulay, the compla-cent pride of J. R. Green in the exploits of freedom-loving Teutonic ancestors; and that any statement of the European, and especially of the Latin interpretation of events, let alone a statement made with a defiantly corrective over-emphasis, must have caused a seismic intellectual shock. It is pro-foundly disturbing (and disagreeable) to be made to feel that axioms of that national mythology which one has always taken for granted are capable of contradiction; and the process provokes a correspondingly profound resentment. It may be partly for this reason that Belloc's moving, solid, personal visualizations of history have met with a hostility that never seriously threatened, say, Lytton Strachey's highly selective portraits, or even Philip Guedalla's conversation-pieces in the glossy convention of Winterhalter. *A propos* of his historical work it may be apposite to quote Belloc's own remarks (in a contribution to *The English Way*) upon St. Thomas Becket. 'All challengers', he writes, 'suffer of necessity the temptations of pride. They are of the breed of certitude and of simplicity' and they 'cannot but be of that human sort which is imperfect through aggression and assertiveness and edge'. Here is, perhaps, as good an indication of the quality of Belloc the historian, as is the following passage from his sketch of Villon of the quality of Belloc the writer in general. 'His vigour ... is all about him and through him, like a storm in a wood. It creates, it perceives. It possesses the man himself and us also as we read him.'

This sketch, part of the delightful *Avril; Essays on the Poetry of the French Renaissance*, exemplifies another, and too small a branch of his activity: literary criticism.

There are also the books of travel, mostly on foot or under sail. They are marked by two characteristics: by an enduring awareness of that historical past which quivers like the last vibrations of a bell within all the landscapes, cities, and seas of the Old World; and by an acute sense of present, immediate, visual significance, a sense which bursts now and then even out of the sentences which so powerfully and so transparently contain it, into quick, accurate, evocative drawings.

There are the many volumes of essays, multitudinous, stimulating, irritating, reminiscent, various, as good talk.

Finally, and perhaps more lasting than all the rest, there are the poems; alive with that energy with which a formal verse structure can most fully be charged; and written to reach the heart through hearing as well as the mind's eye by the provocation of visual imagery. It is to be noted that just as drawings flower out of Belloc's prose, so tunes break through to take command of his songs. It is a pity that his own airs for 'Tarantella' and 'The Winged Horse' and 'Ha'nacker Hill', to name only a few of them, are not reproduced in the collected edition of *Sonnets and Verse*, for they belong so essentially to the words and to the man, as any can vouch who have heard them sung, even by the ghost of a voice on a gramophone record, the ghost of a voice, thin, clear, still true in old age.

Here then is a brief and necessarily over-simplified general account of Belloc's exuberant and varied work. The wood is mapped, now to look at the trees.

II

In considering the books of mockery it is to be remembered that the incidentals of laughter belong to passing time, and are as clearly shaped by their period as are fashions in clothes. Their newness, their relevance, their exquisite immediacy must necessarily fade with the moment they illuminate. This is what has happened to Belloc's satirical novels, even though they were illustrated by G. K. Chesterton. It has happened the more thoroughly in that they are almost pure narrative, showing little of that awareness of physical landscape which is continually present in so much of his other work. The characters, the backgrounds, the situations upon which his embittered high spirits played were—and are—as topical as the hobble skirt and the cloche hat. They are, moreover, separated from contemporary experience not so much by years as by an immense and widening gulf of social change. Remote as *Charley's Aunt*[1] for instance are the figures of merry undergraduates, who can resent the refusal of their fathers to pay gambling debts to the tune of thousands of pounds.

It is not so with the direct caricatures, fundamentally and immortally comic, in which he presents, with the deep and joyful satisfaction of a naturalist in really fine specimens, characteristic examples of human pretentiousness, pomposity and self-importance. These survive ever green. Perhaps the Nordic Man (from *Short Talks with the Dead*) has a slightly Edwardian cut to his jib; but how charmingly recognizable he still is as 'The Conquerer and the Adventurer . . . the Lawgiver and the Essentially Moral Man . . . extremely particular about shaving . . . very reserved, save in the matter of speech-making' and detesting 'all ostentation in dress, and . . . even more the wearing of cheap clothes'. Dr. Caliban's conscientious and ponderous *Guide to Letters*, with its grand financial hypocrisies and its admirable advice on the composition of Reviews, Personal Pars,

[1] The ever-popular farce by Brandon Thomas, first produced in 1892.

Topographical Articles, Political Appeals and the rest, is perennially delightful reading, especially the chapters on Poetry and Interviewing. The first provides a number of exercises in various styles, some—notably the Obscure— still extant, though the Prattling (as follows) has mercifully had its utterance choked in the dust of late Victorian anthologies :

> Little tasteless Pimpernel
> Shepherd's Holt and warning spell
> Crouching in the cushat shade
> Like a mond of mowry made . . .

The chapter on Interviewing is agreeable for its inspired grip of *clichés*, its unctuous quotations from a fustian Old Testament writer whose cadences are undeniably Jacobean ('better is he that humbleth himself than a pillar of brass, and a meek heart than many fastenings') and for those flashes of glorious unexpectedness in which the reader, treading suddenly a non-existent stair, comprehends such a sentence as 'here he reverently raised the plain billycock hat which he is in the habit of wearing in his drawingroom'.

Lambkin's Remains, an equally solemn biography of an imaginary Don, is a perpetual feast to all whose palates have savoured the pomps of a minor erudition, kept conscientiously up to date ; these will return to roll around their tongues Lambkin's Address to the League of Progress, Lambkin's Open Letter to Churchmen, 'Am I a Sheep or a Goat?', the remarks of his biographer upon 'a fine old Arabic poem (I mean the Comedy which we are accustomed to call the Book of Job)', Lambkin's own exquisitely philosophical and tautologous essays on Success and on Sleep, and of course Lambkin's Newdigate Poem with its classical Second Invocation to the Muse:

> Descend O Muse, from thy divine abode
> To Osney on the Seven Bridges Road
> For under Osney's solitary shade
> The bulk of the Electric Light is made.

This leads to that realm of shrewd abandon (more *terre à terre* than Edward Lear's nonsense, more brutal than Lewis Carroll's) inhabited by Bad and Worse Children, Beasts, Peers, Ladies and Gentlemen, and the heroes and heroines of the *Moral Alphabet* and *Cautionary Tales*. These were, of course, part of a reaction against Victorian didacticism, a reaction also to be found in Harry Graham's *Ruthless Rhymes for Heartless Homes*.

> Father heard his children scream
> So he threw them in the stream
> Saying, as he drowned the third
> 'Children should be seen, not heard.'

They were in fact *pastiches* of a kind of verse once written in all seriousness for the instruction and edification of the young. But who now remembers the gentle Ann and Jane Taylor[1] and their warning stories of 'Dirty Jim' and 'Meddlesome Matty'; or even the rhymes gloating on the fate of Augustus who died of refusing to eat his soup, Fidgety Phil, Harriet and the Matches and Little Suck a Thumb? 'The wind has blown them all away', and the last lot were a good riddance; but it is curious that the originals should disappear while the parodies which sprang from them remain, and glow with an immortality all their own. Who forgets Franklin Hyde 'carousing in the dirt', Henry King's untimely death, the lachrymose Lord Lundy, or the virtuous 'George Augustus Fortescue' who ultimately

> . . . married Fifi, only child
> Of Bunyan, first Lord Aberfylde
> And built 'The Cedars', Muswell Hill
> Where he resides in affluence still
> To show what everybody might
> Become by Simply Doing Right.

Faintly in this last, as loudly in *Mrs. Markham's New History of England*, echoes the snarling trumpet which mocks

---

[1] Jane (1783-1824) and Ann Taylor (1782-1866) authors of works for the young.

triumphant and conscious virtue in its meditative self-congratulation, and exposes for what they are 'the easy speeches that comfort cruel men'.

III

It may seem irrelevant to touch upon sociology in a sketch primarily devoted to letters ; but a living body of writing cannot be divided into watertight compartments, and it is essential to indicate the structure of thought implicit in all its activities.   Belloc's sociological beliefs may briefly be outlined thus.   That 'widely distributed property as a condition of freedom is necessary to the normal satisfaction of human nature'.   That in the high Middle Ages, by the time that peasants had come to own and farm their land, and manufacture and trade were organized by self-governing guilds dedicated to God, an approach to such a life existed. That it could only continue and flourish under a strong centralized monarchy holding and using its power to protect the small man.   That the acquisition of monastery lands by a number of powerful families after the Reformation began to sap the royal power, which subsequently dwindled, struggling, until its temporary extinction during the Great Rebellion of the seventeenth century.   That it flared up again for two more reigns, but was finally crushed out by the Glorious Revolution of 1688, when rich men got rid of the last King to exert real power, and installed a foreign puppet who would carry out their desires.   That because the industrial revolution, a process in itself morally neutral, occurred first in a country governed by an oligarchy concerned with the acquisition of abstract wealth and power rather than with the production and use of concrete objects, it brought about an evil and inhuman oppression of the poor, already cheated out of the lands they held by traditional tenure, through the passage of Acts of Parliament confiscating all holdings of whose ownership no written proof existed. That the event known as 'the glorious palladium of our liberties' was in fact the glorious palladium of the liberty of the powerful to exploit the weak; and that, in order to restore a fully human life to the vast majority of Britain's twentieth-century population, it was necessary first to realize with humility in what miserable helplessness and frustration they lived, and then to take strong measures completely to alter the structure of society.

The historical justification of these beliefs is put forward in a number of narratives and biographies. A statement of the current situation, and of alternatives for the future, is made in *The Servile State* (1912), a remarkable prophecy of economic totalitarianism. Plans for the restoration of that individual economic independence which is the only solid basis for individual political liberty are outlined in a number of pamphlets and articles and in several books. *Economics for Helen* (1924) sets the claims of freedom and responsibility against those advantages of personal security and general stability which the Servile State may give. *An Essay on the Restoration of Property* (1936), distinguishes between the Distributist and the Social Credit proposals (remarking that the ultimate end of the former is economic freedom, and of the latter increased purchasing power), advocates various means of distributing ownership in land, shops, and collective enterprises, and postulates that there will be no middle way for the future between general small ownership and general (unlabelled) industrial slavery.

Some of these theories were already distastefully familiar in the peaceful, safe, comfortable educated England of forty years ago, as formulated and iterated from the Marxist point of view; notably those concerned with the exploitation of the weak, the meaninglessness of political liberty without economic power, and the complete inadequacy of the liberal tradition to handle industrial problems. That they should be put forward from a fresh angle, by a man bred up in the Christian tradition and indeed appealing to it, outraged all those who had quietly accepted the belief that their country, 'broadening down from precedent to precedent', was the leader of mankind in its inevitable progress towards perfection.   The theories and the proposals were received with that thick, muffling, stifling silence which is the most potent and most infuriating of all defences against unwelcome argument.

Belloc, whose English mother, descended from that uncompromising Unitarian Joseph Priestley, had spent her youth in the unpopular nineteenth-century struggle for the emancipation of women; Belloc whose French forefathers had fought in the Revolutionary wars, continued to reiterate his convictions; but there became apparent a note of strain and exasperation, as of one who shouts perpetually at those who are deaf because they will not hear.

IV

It is perhaps for this reason that his earlier historical work— among which should be counted biography as well as narra- tive—and indeed all the historical studies dealing with France rather than with England, are the most leisured, stimulating and agreeable.   They carry no sense of angry, anguished urgency, of over-simplified pattern, no implicit appeal to listen before it grows too late.   They are written with a detachment that does not preclude decision (duly acknowledged as personal) on disputed points.   They are marked by that intense awareness of interlocking time, place, and personality which is oddly enough lacking in the novels.   Their style and matter are determined by a passion to write of events as they were originally known, not by hearsay or headline, but in terms of human experience; the years measured by a man's memory, a lifetime, a span of generations; the battles seen not as names on a map, but as the struggles of men, fighting, retreating, advancing in given landscapes dominated by woods or mountains and intersected by roads and rivers, or in the changing winds and tides and currents of the sea.   The heavy decisions are made, the consequences taken not by general nouns ('the Army', 'the Staff') nor by abstractions ('the trend of thought', 'the spirit of the age', 'economic currents', 'the course of events') but by actual men, men of free will, men stupid, wise, energetic, slow, good, bad, or indifferent. In all this Belloc, who, brought up as a young Englishman, nevertheless retained his French nationality until 1911, profited by an experience unshared by his contemporaries in this country; a year's conscript service with the French artillery. Drilling, marching, riding, looking after horses and guns, camping, cooking, singing songs in chorus at the end of the long day, he knew, if not war, its background, and the men called upon to make it.

In *The Eyewitness* (1908) he deliberately set himself at the attempt 'to live for some moments in the past, and to see the things that had been stand and live before one'. He succeeded. The past was illuminated and there lived again in the imagination, as once they were known to perception fragmentarily, sensorily, momentarily, such experiences as the voyage bringing Caesar to Britain, the fight at Roncesvalles, the *Ark Royall's* day and night pursuit of the Spanish Armada with the fireships blown burning along the darkness by the gale, 'the tumbling and foaming sea in a circle all around . . . conspicuous in the strong glare'. In the other historical books this genius for knowing and presenting history in terms of individual human experience is more or less subdued to the stricter discipline of narrative. More, in the distantly focused four-volume *History of England*, and in the *Book of the Bayeux Tapestry*, with its characteristic emphasis on the Norman point of view; less, in the historical biographies, even the *Joan of Arc* written in a stylized archaic prose with Froissart's trumpets sounding round the corners of the paragraphs; least of all in the studies of the French Revolution, in which Belloc's great-grandfather fought. It breaks through and takes charge with particular vigour in the *Robespierre*, the *Marie Antoinette*, and the *Danton*, whose sunset ordeal is described with all the urgency of the present, as, 'waiting his turn without passion', last of a group of friends, he 'heard the repeated fall of the knife in the silence of the crowd'.

V

This deep and vital preoccupation not so much with the material as with the incarnate is indeed a sap perpetually rising within all Belloc's serious work. It animates with especial vigour his books on travel, and because of it they, belonging to a *genre* more liable to dullness (pedantic, diffuse or trivial) than any other, are informed with a triple significance. Mountain and plain and river, town and sea, the exterior landscape in all its strong rhythm and delicate detail, are not only experienced by the limbs and the eyes, not only perceived in terms of that psycho-physical beauty which stimulates and fulfils such vast human longings as those of Wordsworth whom 'the sounding cataract haunted ... like a passion'. Two other things are known through them: the given invisible past; the fluent invisible mind.

Through all his wanderings in England and France and Italy and Algeria and the Pyrenees and Spain and the Baltic, comes the sense of 'it was here' that such a thing happened. Here at Lyme Regis, some three and a half centuries between them, the Black Death and the Duke of Monmouth came ashore. Here 'in these fields' of the Narbonnese was rooted the great landed family from which Charlemagne sprang. The rocks of Roncesvalles re-echo Roland's horn; and the Roman town is still implicit after two thousand years in the layout of Paris, modified then and always by the looping Seine.

Perhaps it is only for the purpose of such an essay as this that all his books of travel are read one after the other; but to do so is to become aware, unmistakably and with some astonishment, of the real root of his temporal loyalty. It does not lie in England, critically loved. It does not lie in

France, loved with the acceptant wonder of childhood and youth. It stretches down into that far older unity which once contained them both. *Civis Romanus sum*; a citizen of that great Rome which died in the Dark Ages, as of Rome reborn in Christendom.

I say a temporal loyalty in order to make it clear that though it is united, in Belloc, with an even more ardent spiritual loyalty to the Catholic Church geographically centred at Rome, the two loyalties are separable and distinct. It is possible to 'feel in one's bones'—and brain—a steady devotion, more, an ineradicable sense of 'belonging' to the traditional life of Europe, in its classical and in its medieval unity, without any conscious allegiance to the Roman Church. It is also possible to confess that Faith without any conscious reference to the classical background within which it first began to grow, or to that first culture-pattern which crystallized around it, an enormous, beautiful, relevant but not essential by-product of its activity in a given time, place, and circumstance. In other times, places circumstances—say the twentieth century, Africa, industrial civilization—its activity will have different material to work on, and the culture-pattern will not be the same. It is the more necessary to stress this point because the impact of Belloc's work—the immense energy, the vitality, the clear and incisive thought, the versatility, the style which carries with the strength of Atlantic breakers all that he has to say—has been so overwhelming as to convince many of his readers that for everyone, as for him, these two loyalties, the temporal and the eternal, cannot be separated. A Jesuit writing as long ago as 1925 pointed out, *à propos* of Belloc's theory that Roman civilization in Britain survived the Saxon invasions, the mistaken readiness of public opinion to believe that 'what Mr. Belloc holds and defends is . . . the view of educated Catholics in general, and possibly . . . inspired by ecclesiastical authority'. It is not so. That would be more than one man could carry.

Belloc's deep temporal loyalty, then, to Rome imperial

as to Rome reborn in the cultural unity of medieval
Christendom, probably explains the bitterness of his antag-
onisms, which are all directed against forces likely to bring
about its disintegration; from the Moslems in North
Africa who cut down the trees Rome planted, and let the
desert in, to the Moslems who fought the Crusaders; from
the Puritans and the Jews (who, harking back, he felt, to
the primitively apprehended idea of God in the Old Testament, seemed to regard financial success as the earnest of
divine approval, and to replace love and contemplation as
the mainspring of living by work and money-making), to
the modern banking system, rendering mechanical, non-
moral, non-just, non-human, automatic, the creative rela-
tionship between men, work, and trade.

Belloc's travels are however not only concerned with the
brimming past and the torrential present of sailing or
trudging, now high-spirited now weary, across France and
Switzerland and Italy, or through the Pyrenees, or over the
South Downs with men talking and quarrelling and singing,
and arguments between Auctor and Lector, and comments
on inns and paths and people. They record an external
and an internal journey in terms of one another. Throughout all his wanderings the outer scene is both a visual delight
in itself and a means of bringing into focus the inner landscape of consciousness. Through its images the mind
becomes aware of and communicates its own experience.
Thus, sailing, he perceives the tides as 'a consequence, a
reflection and a part of the ceaseless pulse and rhythm which
animates all things made'. Again in the great passage
about the sight of the Alps in *The Path to Rome* he sees 'the
sky beyond the edge of the world getting purer as the vault
rose. But right up—a belt in that empyrean—ran peak and
field and needle of intense ice, remote, remote from the
world. . . . From the height of the Weissenstein I saw as it
were my religion. I mean, humility, the fear of death, the
terror of height and of distance, the glory of God, the
infinite potentiality of reception whence springs that divine

thirst of the soul.' And again, of the rejection of belief: 'we are like men who follow down the cleft of a mountain, and the peaks are hidden from us and forgotten. It takes years to reach the dry plain, and then we look back and see our home . . . we who return must suffer hard things, for there grows a gulf between us and many companions. We must once more take up the struggle to reconcile two truths, and to keep civic freedom sacred in spite of the organization of religion.'

If *The Path to Rome*, marked by all the gusto of young manhood, towers above the other books of travel by land, *The Cruise of the 'Nona'*, made with the sense of growing old upon him, is incomparably the best of Belloc's writings on the sea. It follows the pattern outlined above of a simultaneous inner and outer journey. It draws even a conscious parallel between 'the course of a boat and the soul of a man'. In it are recorded, during the 'interstices of sailing', some 'poor scraps of judgement and memory'. It contains none of those cataracts of adjectives and adverbs which burst through his earlier work like volcanic geysers, linking him, oddly enough, with Charles Kingsley, who shared his passion for the style of Rabelais from which they spout up. Its currents carry the shape of thoughts conveyed with distinct animus in much of his other work, but reflected here with the profound peace of ocean, where time itself is 'more continuous; more part of the breathing of the world; less mechanical and divided'. He considers at leisure Fools; History; Words; the Press; the Gentry; the possible breakdown of great communities into little independent ones like 'Ithaca and Corfu and Wight and Kent'; those who take up the cause of subject peoples; and the certain rise of some new religion (though he does not, writing in 1925, know it to be Marxism). Permeating all his argument come the sound and sight and smell of the sea, now fierce, now foggy, now calm, calling for judgement and skill, yielding to wind and sail; the sea where 'a man is nearest to his own making and in communion with that from which he came and to which he shall return', the sea 'the common sacrament of the world' that 'shall comfort us, and perpetually show us new things, and reassure us'.

In this context Mr. Belloc's contentions provoke neither fierce agreement nor violent reaction, but quiet brooding thought. They take on the vast unhurried strength of the tides; and the whole book can be read and re-read with such delight and fulfilment as the very smell and coldness of the waves bring to those who find seafaring (rather than Bacon's garden) 'the purest of human pleasures'.

VI

The essays are so many and various that it is almost impossible to discuss them *en bloc*. They consider with wit, ferocity, learning, personal reminiscence, prejudice, compassion, intolerance, common sense, a wide experience of the outer world and a most noble prose style almost every aspect of individual human life; but they do not touch upon science, technics, or any sort of statistical general-ization. To read them is like dining at ease with a really great conversationalist ; in them the richness and depth of the written word amply replace that air of golden geniality —say the spiritual equivalent of candle-lit cigar-smoke and the lingering vibration of wine—which gives to its spoken counterpart a quality evaporated by print. Some—pro-ducts of his years in Parliament, of his unsuccessful struggle for the public auditing of Party funds, and of the libel action in which his paper, the *New Witness*, was involved just before the first world war—are political and polemical. Others discuss incidental aspects of those main themes with which his large-scale books are concerned: religion, history, social patterns, places, buildings, people. Scattered through them all come remarks on the critical assessment of literature and the close consideration of style, and it is evident that these have been his preoccupation on and off throughout his life as a writer. Enormous though his own output has

been, it becomes clear that its form has never been allowed
simply to determine itself like lava cooling into shape after
a volcanic eruption. Setting verse aside for the moment,
innumerable scattered sentences show that he has been perpetually aware of the various methods and skills and tech-
niques inherent in the writing of good prose. Witness for
instance his remarks in praise of Dr. Johnson, that he 'puts
all there is to say of a considered judgement . . . into the
antithetical form, than which no better medium has ever
been discovered for condensing and preserving a con-
clusion'; his pointing out that where Voltaire's verbal
'economy is like a sphere, the maximum content for its
surface, Johnson's is like strong soup, a concentration of
nourishment'; his condemnation of Milton's 'haggis-
prose of controversy' and his summary 'there are some men
who think that concision is a matter of short words and short
sentences. It is not so. Concision is a matter of giving
what you have to give in the least compass compatible with
lucidity.' His reflections on the rhythms of Tyndale and of
Cranmer, those great Scripture translators, show his recogni-
tion of the power of prose to shape channels of feeling. They
show also a nice discrimination between the kind of prose
which is, as it were, a natural phenomenon, a growing thing
that needs only pruning and training to bring it to perfection;
and the kind that is deliberately willed, made, carefully and
slowly, painfully chiselled by the conscious mind from un-
wieldy boulders of hard, compressed, unformulated thought.
Cranmer's exquisite style was, he contends, of the latter
sort. The 'utility-diction', so to speak, of his letters, was
as clumsy and tautologous as that of most sixteenth-century
English correspondence. It was only when he set himself
down to his great work, the Prayer Book liturgy, whose
cadences were to evoke and to echo Anglican devotion for
hundreds of years, that he became 'a jeweller in prose'.
Belloc's own magnificent English should be less read
about than read ; and preferably read aloud. It is not only
a flexible and sensitive and precise instrument for conveying

meaning. It can give to the listener a shock of auditory
pleasure like that shock of visual delight with which un-
erring draughtsmanship is seen.

A group of admirers have, indeed, modelled their own
writings upon its clarity, its muscular rhythm, and its gusto.
Few of them, however, have been sustained by an impulse
of such strength as Belloc's 'spouting well of joy within
that never yet was dried'; and occasionally, as happens
with all 'schools', the followers have tended to exaggerate
even to caricaturing point the characteristics of their chosen
master. In serious writing they have been apt to enlarge
and over-simplify outline and emotion, and to overwork
and make hackneyed such adjectives as 'great' as a numi-
nous equivalent for 'large' or even 'big'; and in loose-
limbed comedy or knockabout satire to force high spirits
to such a pitch that one at least of them has been very
properly reproached with talking through Mr. Belloc's
hat. *Le style c'est l'homme*; but *l'homme* is in the singular.

Where verse is concerned, Belloc's critical work is chiefly
to be found in *Avril*, the series of essays on the poetry of the
French Renaissance, written in 1904 in the hope that English
ignorance of French literature and life were on the wane,
and that England and France might begin to understand one
another better: in *Milton*, written in 1935, where deliberate
attention to Milton's position as 'the national poet' whose
genius set the stamp of Protestantism on English culture,
keeps yielding to a passionate discriminating interest in his
poetic technique, and a craftsman's admiration of its achieve-
ments; and, in a negative form, in *Caliban's Guide to
Letters*, already briefly discussed among the books of
mockery. Incidentally, it is odd to observe how often the
poem 'The Yellow Mustard' from this hilarious volume is
included without comment in collections of Belloc's own
serious verse, whereas context and content show it to be a
pastiche of the work of a late-Victorian poetaster.

Avril surveys with love the work of six French poets of
the fifteenth and sixteenth centuries. To each is devoted

an essay, followed by a number of his verses, with brief
commentaries.   It is very right that the first of them should
be Charles d'Orléans who, taken prisoner after Agincourt,
wrote most of his poems during his twenty-five years of
captivity in England.   Two of them, '*Dieu qu'il la fait bon
regarder, La gracieuse bonne et belle*' and the prayer for the
soul of his wife in purgatory, remain as long in the remem-
brance as Ronsard's '*Quand tu seras bien vieille, le soir a la
chandelle*'; Du Bellay's epitaphs on his Dog Peloton and
his Cat Belaud, and Villon's ballade of the Dead Ladies and
his lesser known rondeau epitaph for himself, returning
upon the dying fall of

> *Repos eternal don a cil*
> *Sire, et clarté perpetuel.*

In his consideration of this poetry Belloc is concerned
with the themes of enjoyment, energy, and form.   He
surveys in its chronological development the change from
the spring freshness of medieval lyric, simple in impulse
if complex in verbal pattern, to the summer strength
of classicism canalizing 'a torrent which, undisciplined,
would serve but to destroy'.   He concludes that 'energy
alone can dare to be classical.   Where the great currents of
the soul run feebly a perpetual acceleration . . . will be
demanded ; where they run full and heavy, then under the
restraint of form they will but run more proudly and more
strong.'   This indeed is his defence against the Romantics,
of the last of his poets, Malherbe, whose own creative
work may not be found memorable, but who consciously
set up—or clamped down—definite canons of style in
French literature.   Against comparison with the unself-
conscious if ingenious earlier poetry there can be no defence,
but only regret.   It is the difference between youth and
maturity, song and orchestration.   Curiously, Belloc himself does not seem to be sensible of this inevitable change as
of a loss, either in the present volume or in the study of
Milton, though he notes that the lyric impulse died in that

poet when he was twenty-nine. It may be of course that
the desire wholly to return to those unsullied springs comes
from a lack of strength and perseverance enough to compre-
hend the deep rivers to which they give rise, and is part of
that sick love of the primitive which means that some faculty
has withered in the ripening. In his own poetry, Belloc
uses every form but formlessness, handling with skill not
only the sonnet and epigram and quatrain to which the
English eye and ear are accustomed, but also the rhymed
couplet, seldom employed since Dryden's time to carry any
sustained emotion but anger and humour; and the charac-
teristically medieval form of the ballade, employed in the
medieval manner to convey not the ornamental bric-à-brac
fancies with which Alfred Austin could load it, but genuine
emotion diverse in satire tenderness or prayer, as in the
Ballade of Our Lady of Czestowa and the sardonic, moving
Envoi to the Ballade of Unsuccessful Men :

> . . . Prince, may I venture, since it's only you
> To speak discreetly of the Crucified?
> He was extremely unsuccessful, too:
> The Devil didn't like Him, and He died.

Where *Avril* is concerned with the verse of a group or
French poets writing at a time when Europe was still united
in all its diversity, *Milton*, set in an age of differentiated and
self-assertive nationalism, deals with one man and his marmoreal work; a man linked by learning and 'the antique
worship of beauty' with that classical Rome in which
Belloc's own roots are set; linked with this country by
'that prime English characteristic—vivid visual imagination' and also alas by that conviction which he was the
first to formulate, that whenever God has anything impor-
tant to impart to the world He first confides it to 'His
Englishmen'; and linked with Puritanism by historical
circumstance, family friction, and personal pride. Although
the events, activity, thought of his individual life, the bitterness of solitude and frustrated affection and physical blind-

ness, the furious fulminations on divorce and other pamphlet themes, the long, final, unpublished swing towards Arianism, are clearly outlined against the insecure political and economic background, the final impression left is that all this was of importance chiefly as the husk-experience whence his verse could spring. The volume is full of reflections on the nature and technique of poetry. 'Very good verse may be compared to a young horse, off and away ... who now and then seems to stumble, but is right again in a split second.' 'Lucidity in verse as in prose is the very soul of the matter.' 'Sound is primary.' 'The Sonnet is not a cry, nor the voice of an emotion; it is a thing made, and made slowly, an exercise in verse by man, creator of his own world.' Belloc contends that although Milton had no clear idea of the break that should exist between the octet and the sestet of the sonnet, a break as between statement and comment, question and reply, a phrase in music and its fulfilment, he achieved perfection in this form in the sonnet on the Massacre of the Waldenses, which he praises as 'complete in its noise and its meaning from its surface to its depths, in its under and in its over tones'. He discusses the epics, with their 'classic sense of form' and 'fixed striving after the sublime'; and dwells with long relish on the varied sequence of sound from 'linkéd sweetness long drawn out' to the gongs of celestial war and such short syllable phrases as what he calls 'the drum beat of "The African" ' ($\bar{u}\,\bar{u}\,\breve{u}\,\breve{u}$). He savours also, to the full, Milton's 'masterly use of the place-name', 'that cymbal the place-name'. This love of place-names, relating poetry to one or another single, definite, unique, actual locality is of course part of that passion for things incarnate which has already been noted. The sonorous name, even of somewhere unknown, is an earnest of something knowable, in all its strangeness, to sense and spirit; whether it is that of Alph the sacred river, of 'Ormuzd or of Ind' or of Samarkand or Flores in the Azores, of Eigg or Mull or Skye or of those English places in which the aerial of vision is earthed, cited in

> Lift up your hearts in Gumber, laugh the Weald
> And you my mother the valley of Arun sing

and . . . 'once atop of Lambourne down toward the hill of
Clere' and . . . 'Yarnton's tiny docks of stone' upon

> The tender Evenlode that makes
> Her meadows hush to hear the sound
> Of waters mingling in the brakes
> And binds my heart to English ground.

These last quotations are of course from Belloc's own
poems; and one reason why the books of literary criticism
have been discussed at what may seem to be disproportionate
length is because their conclusions are so clearly drawn from
and applicable to his own work, the reflections of a man who
has struggled and wrestled with obdurate words, as a
sculptor with stone, until they were subdued to carry
meaning in grace.

VII

Belloc's poems, like his prose, are of many kinds. The
comic ones have already been discussed. There are also
the furious grotesques such as 'The Happy Journalist' and
'To Dives' and those lines to the

> Remote and ineffectual Don
> That dared attack my Chesterton

which almost orchestrate the splutter of rage.

There are the songs, some with their own airs, and each
springing from a single mood, spontaneous as a child dancing
irresistibly along on a sunny morning, or kicking through
autumn leaves. Among them are the splendid 'The
Winged Horse'; 'Tarantella', full of the noise of casta-
nets stilled suddenly to sadness and 'the boom, Of the far
waterfall like Doom'; the regretful 'Sally is gone that
was so kindly'; 'Beyond the Islands' with its primitive
Hebridean cadence; 'When I was not much older, Than
Cupid, but bolder . . .' the only piece of verse in which
Belloc has used a late eighteenth-century mode; and

several drinking songs. There are some carols, their imagery vivid as that of medieval illumination; and some short poems devoted to the statement of visual impressions, like those flat Chinese paintings of a bough, a heron, or a clump of reeds, which present fact and imply feeling. Of this sort are the four lines beginning 'The moon on the one hand, the dawn on the other'. There are also the straightforward active poems like the 'Dedicatory Ode', and 'The South Country' and the 'Stanzas on Battersea Bridge in a southwesterly gale'.

Among the more deliberately wrought work are the ballades, already touched upon; the epigrams; the sonnets; and the 'Heroic Poem in Praise of Wine'.

The epigrams have that bronze brevity which is the soul not only of wit but of immediate emotion. One or two are compliments, set forth with skilful elegance. Many engrave a hatred in two lines, or pack sardonic comment into four. Some employ brute force; witness 'On His Books', 'The Pacifist', 'On Mundane Acquaintance' and 'On a Puritan':

> He served his God so faithfully and well
> That now he meets him face to face, in hell.

Others embody an austere tenderness perhaps most perfectly shown in 'The Statue':

> When we are dead, some Hunting-boy will pass
> And find a stone half hidden in tall grass
> And grey with age; but having seen that stone
> (Which was your image), ride more slowly on.

Yet others brim over with that enhanced sense of mortality inseparable from the love of living; and here (at last) may be quoted the Fifty-first epigram, one of a series on a sundial:

> Here in a lonely glade, forgotten, I
> Mark the tremendous process of the sky.
> So does your inmost soul, forgotten, mark
> The Dawn, the Noon, the coming of the Dark.

The sonnets, of which there are thirty-eight, cannot be assessed in such a short space as remains. They are to be read, repeatedly; first tasting meaning and sound, and presently with full pleasure in their style. The first, the fifteenth, the sixteenth and the wonderful eighteenth and twenty-sixth should be read above all.

Perhaps it is because Belloc is experienced both in satire and in laughter that he can use simultaneously and with success two modes of expression either of which is particularly liable in the English idiom to corrosion by ridicule: rhetoric and the rhymed couplet. Both are employed with moving and resounding effect in that 'Heroic Poem in Praise of Wine' which is his greatest single creative achievement. Its setting, its imagery, its final passages which can move reader and hearer to unexpected tears, exemplify in perfection the poet's loyalty to ancient Rome and Rome reborn. This too must be read, and read aloud, from its first theme, wine itself, and the dancing procession of Dionysus to plant the vines in Europe, to its culmination in the Christian hour of death:

Strong brother in God, and last companion, Wine.

VIII

The stronger a man's impact is on his time, the more difficult it is immediately to assess. Belloc's ideas have never, like those of his contemporaries Shaw and Wells, been so completely assimilated into current opinion as to become taken for granted, axiomatic, anonymous presuppositions. They are still exterior and irritant to the main body of our culture. The very vehemence with which his political theories have been put forward has probably made them rebound from a general consciousness tightening itself, as it were, to repel judgements that might bruise too seriously that collective self-esteem necessary to group survival. Nevertheless, as the vast structure of industrial capitalism changes, crumbles or collapses, it may be recollected that Belloc saw and detested as vividly as any Marxist its vast injustices and its advertising-slogan self-justifications; and that he put forward a remedy conceived in terms of constructive human happiness instead of one based upon the misery of mechanized mass-revolution. He has shown that it is possible to interpret history in accordance with another pattern than that conventionally propounded and accepted; and he has through all his writings made plain to an England perhaps less insular than she was fifty years ago the ancient unity of the Roman Empire, of medieval Christendom, and of the European tradition, to which she too belongs.

He has probably added a new type to the popular concept of the Catholic in this country, placing beside a sinister, silent, intriguing, rather uncanny indoor figure that of a burly man singing, shouting, arguing, and drinking beer in the open air. His comic verses, more particularly perhaps *The Bad Child's Book of Beasts* and *More Beasts for Worse Children* have lit laughter in three generations, and have had a host of imitators, some gloriously successful. His serious poems have kept too close to the classical canons of objectivity, formality, and lucidity to attract fashionable literary attention during a half-century whose predominant interest has been in subjective vision, the abandonment of convention and the pursuit of experiment both in the manner and in the matter of verse. Nevertheless, their splendour is becoming known, outside as well as inside England; and their influence in matters of technique may fairly be traced in the work of poets as diverse as Roy Campbell and Martyn Skinner.

Belloc's prose will probably survive in part, to give enlarging joy to lovers of pre-industrial Europe and the sea. But in his poems will rest his immortality and the fulfilment of his outrageous and heartfelt pun:

> When I am dead I hope it may be said
> "His sins were scarlet but his books were read."

HILAIRE BELLOC

A Select Bibliography

(Place of publication London, unless stated otherwise.)

Collected Editions:

A PICKED COMPANY (1915).

A selection from the Writings.

SONNETS AND VERSE (1923).

Revised 1928. New edition with additional poems and an Introduction by R. Jebb, 1954.

SELECTED ESSAYS (1926).

SELECTIONS FROM HUMOROUS WRITINGS (1935).

STORIES, ESSAYS, AND POEMS (1938).

ON SAILING THE SEA (1939).

A collection of sea-going writings.

CAUTIONARY VERSES (1940).

THE SILENCE OF THE SEA (1941).

Essays selected by W. N. Roughead.

SELECTED ESSAYS (1948).

Introduction by J. B. Morton.

SELECTED CAUTIONARY VERSES (1950).

AN ANTHOLOGY OF PROSE AND VERSE (1951).

Selected by W. N. Roughead.

SONGS OF THE SOUTH COUNTRY (1951).

Separate Works:

VERSES AND SONNETS (1896). *Verse.*

THE BAD CHILD'S BOOK OF BEASTS (1896). *Verse.*

MORE BEASTS—FOR WORSE CHILDREN (1897). *Verse.*

THE LIBERAL TRADITION (1897). *Essays.*

THE MODERN TRAVELLER (1898). *Verse.*

A MORAL ALPHABET (1899). *Verse.*

DANTON (1899). *Biography.*

LAMBKIN'S REMAINS (1900). *Pastiche.*

PARIS (1900). *History.*

ROBESPIERRE (1901). *Biography.*

THE PATH TO ROME (1902). *Travel.*

CALIBAN'S GUIDE TO LETTERS (1903).　*Pastiche.*

AVRIL (1904).　*Criticism.*

EMMANUEL BURDEN (1904).　*Political Satire.*

THE OLD ROAD (1904).　*Travel.*

ESTO PERPETUA (1906).　*Travel.*

THE HILLS AND THE SEA (1906).　*Essays.*

THE HISTORIC THAMES (1907).　*Topography.*

CAUTIONARY TALES (1907).　*Verse.*

ON NOTHING (1908).　*Essays.*

THE EYE WITNESS (1908).　*History.*

MR. CLUTTERBUCK'S ELECTION (1908).　*Novel.*

THE PYRENEES (1909).　*Travel.*

ON EVERYTHING (1909).　*Essays.*

A CHANGE IN THE CABINET (1909).　*Novel.*

MARIE ANTOINETTE (1909).　*Biography.*

ON ANYTHING (1910).　*Essays.*

PONGO AND THE BULL (1910).　*Novel.*

VERSES (1910).　*Verse.*

ON SOMETHING (1910).　*Essays.*

MORE PEERS (1911).　*Comic Verse.*

THE GIRONDIN (1911).　*Novel.*

THE PARTY SYSTEM (with Cecil Chesterton) (1911).　*Political discussion.*

FIRST AND LAST (1911).　*Essays.*

THE FRENCH REVOLUTION (1911).　*History.*

WARFARE IN ENGLAND (1912).　*History.*

THE FOUR MEN (1912).　*Travel.*

THE GREEN OVERCOAT (1912).　*Novel.*

THE SERVILE STATE (1912).　*Sociology.*

THE RIVER OF LONDON (1912).　*Topography.*

THIS AND THAT AND THE OTHER (1912).　*Essays.*

THE STANE STREET (1913).　*Travel.*

THE BOOK OF THE BAYEUX TAPESTRY (1914).　*History.*

CONTINUATION OF LINGARD'S HISTORY (1914).　*History.*

THE EUROPEAN WAR: FIRST PHASE (1915).　*History.*

THE EUROPEAN WAR: SECOND PHASE (1916).　*History.*

THE LAST DAYS OF FRENCH MONARCHY (1916).　*History.*

THE FREE PRESS (1918).　*Sociology.*

THE PRINCIPLES OF WAR (1918). *History.*

EUROPE AND THE FAITH (1920). *Religion.*

THE HOUSE OF COMMONS AND THE MONARCHY (1920). *Politics.*

THE JEWS (1922). *Essay.*

THE MERCY OF ALLAH (1922). *Linked short stories.*

ON (1923). *Essays.*

THE CONTRAST (between Europe and America) (1923). *Essay.*

THE CAMPAIGN OF 1812 AND THE RETREAT FROM MOSCOW (1924). *History.*

ECONOMICS FOR HELEN (1924). *Economics.*

HISTORY OF ENGLAND, Vols. I and II (1925). *History.*

HISTORY OF ENGLAND, Vol. III (1928). *History.*

HISTORY OF ENGLAND, Vol. IV (1932). *History.*

THE CRUISE OF THE 'NONA' (1925). *Travel.*

New edition, with an Introduction by Lord Stanley of Alderley, 1955.

MR. PETRE (1925). *Novel.*

MINIATURES OF FRENCH HISTORY (1925). *History.*

THE EMERALD OF CATHERINE THE GREAT (1926). *Novel.*

A COMPANION TO MR. WELLS'S OUTLINE OF HISTORY (1926). *Historica criticism.*

MR. BELLOC STILL OBJECTS TO MR. WELLS'S OUTLINE OF HISTORY (1926). *Historical criticism.*

A reply to *Mr. Belloc Objects to the Outline of History* by H. G. Wells (1926).

MRS. MARKHAM'S NEW HISTORY OF ENGLAND (1926). *Satire.*

SHORT TALKS WITH THE DEAD (1926). *Essays.*

THE HAUNTED HOUSE (1927). *Novel.*

JAMES THE SECOND (1928). *Biography.*

MANY CITIES (1928). *Travel.*

BUT SOFT, WE ARE OBSERVED (1928). *Novel.*

A CONVERSATION WITH AN ANGEL (1928). *Essays.*

HOW THE REFORMATION HAPPENED (1928). *History.*

WHERE ARE THE DEAD? (1928). *Essays.*

Including a contribution by Belloc.

BELINDA (1928). *Novel.*

SURVIVALS AND NEW ARRIVALS (1929). *Essays.*

JOAN OF ARC (1929). *Biography.*

THE MISSING MASTERPIECE (1929). *Novel.*

RICHELIEU (1929).   *Biography.*

THE MAN WHO MADE GOLD (1930).   *Novel.*

WOLSEY (1930).   *Biography.*

NEW CAUTIONARY TALES (1930).   *Verse.*

CROMWELL (1931).   *Biography.*

CRANMER (1931).   *Biography.*

ON TRANSLATION.   Oxford (1931).   *Taylorian Lecture.*

A CONVERSATION WITH A CAT (1931).   *Essays.*

NINE NINES OR NOVENAS FROM A CHINESE LITANY OF OLD NUMBERS (1931).
   Miscellany.

SIX BRITISH BATTLES (1931).   *History.*

THE POSTMASTER GENERAL (1932).   *Novel.*

NAPOLEON (1932).   *Biography.*

ESSAYS OF A CATHOLIC (1932).   *Essays.*

AN HEROIC POEM IN PRAISE OF WINE (1932).   *Verse.*

CHARLES THE FIRST: KING OF ENGLAND (1933).   *Biography.*

BECKETT (1933).   *Biography.*

THE TACTICS AND STRATEGY OF THE GREAT DUKE OF MARLBOROUGH
   (1933).   *History.*

WILLIAM THE CONQUEROR (1933).   *Biography.*

A SHORTER HISTORY OF ENGLAND (1934).   *History.*

MILTON (1935).   *Biography.*

AN ESSAY ON THE RESTORATION OF PROPERTY (1936).   *Essay.*

THE COUNTY OF SUSSEX (1936).   *Travel.*

THE BATTLE GROUND: A HISTORY OF SYRIA TO 1187 A.D. (1936).   *History*

THE HEDGE AND THE HORSE (1936).   *Novel.*

THE CRUSADE (1937).   *History.*

CHARACTERS OF THE REFORMATION (1937).   *History.*

THE CRISIS OF OUR CIVILIZATION (1937).   *Sociology.*

AN ESSAY ON THE NATURE OF CONTEMPORARY ENGLAND (1937).
   Sociology.

MONARCHY (LOUIS XIV) (1938).   *History.*

THE QUESTION AND THE ANSWER (1938).   *Explanation of Catholic belief.*

RETURN TO THE BALTIC (1938).   *Travel.*

THE GREAT HERESIES (1938). *Theological history.*

THE LAST RALLY (1940). *History.*

ON THE PLACE OF GILBERT CHESTERTON IN ENGLISH LETTERS (1940). *Valediction.*

PLACES (1942). *Essays.*

ELIZABETHAN COMMENTARY (1942). *History.*

Some Biographical and Critical Studies:

HILAIRE BELLOC: NO ALIENATED MAN by F. Wilhelmsen (1954).

HILAIRE BELLOC: A MEMOIR by J. B. Morton (1955).

TESTIMONY TO HILAIRE BELLOC by E. and R. Jebb (1956).

THE LIFE OF HILAIRE BELLOC by R. Speaight (1956).